FLOWERS MADE EASY

THIS BOOK BELONGS TO

• •

_____

_____

inprint

FLOWERS MADE EASY

FLOWERS LIST

THE FLOWER DESIGNS

Every design in this book is origional and
was created to make drawing flowers fun and simple.
Express your own creativity while learning to draw.

WHAT YOU NEED

To get the full benefits from this book,
all you need is a pencil, some paper, and an eraser,
THAT'S IT!

You will be drawing beautiful flowers in minutes.

HOW TO USE THIS BOOK

In the book you will find simple step by step guides that
you can follow along. The first half of the book will
show you every step to each flower,
and the second half has pre-made guides
that you can draw directly onto.
This technique is more enjoyable and efficient
when learning how to draw flowers.

First, get familiar with the flower you would like to draw
by looking at the guide and explanations,
then head over to the practice section
and draw out the steps for yourself.
Use the notes section to write down how easy or hard
that particular flower was for you and what you'd like to improve.
Remember, practice makes perfect.

After you have used every guide,
get a seperate piece of paper and draw out the guides
for yourself, then recreate the steps again until
you have mastered your flower drawing skills!

ANEMONE

GUIDE

1. Draw a circle.
2. Mark the center and divide into 5.
TIP: Think of a star ★ or a starfish
to help you to get the right balance.
3. Draw a small circle in the center.

STEP 1.

1. Draw a small circle in the center.
2. Fill it in with short lines going
around as shown.

STEP 2.

1. Fill the small guide circle with lines
coming out from the center.
2. Add dots on the end of each line.
3. Add smaller dots around them.

STEP 3.

1. Draw a petal on each guideline. Make them like a rounded diamond shape as shown..

STEP 4.

1. Draw petals inbetween the previous 5.
2. Stay inside the guide circle!

STEP 5.

1. Add details petal by petal. Draw lines coming out of the center.
2. Add a few lines near the top of each petal as shown.

DONE!

ANTHURIUM

GUIDE

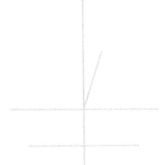

1. Draw a vertical line.
2. Add 2 horizontal lines as shown.
4. Draw a short diagonal line coming out from the center cross section

STEP 1.

Draw this curved line, imagine an upside down heart shape.
Use the guide as shown.

STEP 2.

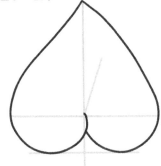

Draw the other side of the heart.

STEP 3.

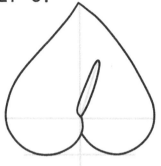

Add a skinny oval shape around the diagonal guideline as shown.

STEP 4.

Draw lines following the shape of the upside down heart to replicate veins of the leaf.

STEP 5.

Draw a stem, and add the details. Start by drawing faint circles inbetween the veins and add lines around them to create shadow.

DONE!

BIRD OF PARADISE

GUIDE

1. Draw the center vertical line.
2. Add 4 more lines spreading out
as shown.

STEP 1.

1. Draw a sharp leaf shape with
a rounded base as shown.
2. Add a line underneath
to start the stem.

STEP 2.

1. Draw the other half of the stem.
2. Add a petal on the right side of
the guide, starting with a straight line
on the top and a curved line
underneth.

STEP 3.

1. Draw a petal in the center..
2. Add another petal on the right and 1 more behind petal ①.

STEP 4.

1. Draw 2 skinny sharp shapes to create what's called the "tongue".

STEP 5.

1. Add details starting with the petals. Draw different length lines from the base and tips.
2. Draw lines on the leaf and the stem.

DONE!

CAMELLIA

GUIDE

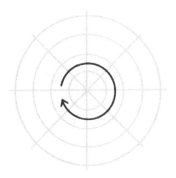

1. Draw the outer circle.
2. Add 3 more circles inside as shown.
3. Divide it into 8 and add faint lines inbetween each section.

*The arrow shows the direction we're going to draw petals.

STEP 1.

1. Draw a short curved line coming out from the middle, then go around the center guide circle creating a shell like shape as shown.
2. Draw 2 curved lines around the "shell" shape.

STEP 2.

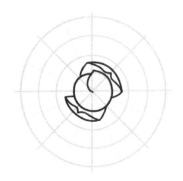

1. Connect the curved lines from STEP 1 to the center of the flower.
2. Add the folded effect to each connected section as shown.

STEP 3.

1. Draw petals starting from the center of the flower.
2. Go around clockwise using the numbers shown.

STEP 4.

1. Keep adding petals one by one, following the numbers shown.

TIP: Vary the sizes as you go.

STEP 5.

1. Add details petal by petal, starting with the center of the flower, make sure the 2 folded petals have more lines to show depth.
2. For the rest of the petals, draw lines in the center from the base, keep the edges clear, and add some detail at the top of each petal as shown.

DONE!

CLEMATIS

GUIDE

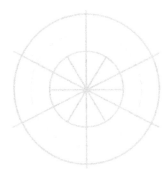

1. Draw the outer circle.
2. Mark the center, and divide it into 6.
3. Draw a smaller circle in the center and divide each section in half as shown.
4. Add an extra faint circle inbetween the previously drawn circles.

STEP 1.

1. Draw a small circle in the center.
2. Add short lines inside, coming from the center as shown.

STEP 2.

Draw a pointy petal using the guide. The widest part of the petal should be on the faint circle as you can see.

STEP 3.

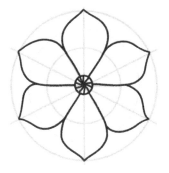

Repeat STEP 2 and draw 5 more petals.

STEP 4.

Draw varied lines from the middle of the flower, staying inside the center guide.

STEP 5.

Add details petal by petal. Draw 3 lines in the center of each petal and add short lines at the edge.

DONE!

CORNFLOWER

GUIDE

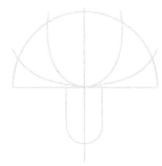

1. Draw a semi circle and add a horizontal line twice the length of the semi circle through the middle.
2. Add a "U" shape underneath.
4. Draw curved lines coming out from the center, as shown.

STEP 1.

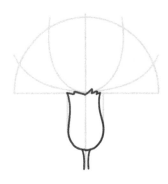

1. Draw this base shape of the flower using the guide.
2. Add a stem.

STEP 2.

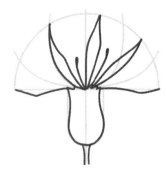

1. Draw 3 skinny pointed petals coming from the base shape.
2. Add 2 pistils with rounded ends inbetween the petals.
4. Draw 2 slightly bent lines along bottom of the semi circle guide as shown.

STEP 3.

1. Turn the last 2 lines from STEP 2 into petals.
2. Add extra petals as shown.

STEP 4.

Fill in the empty spaces until it looks like this.

STEP 5.

1. Add details starting with the base of the flower. Draw scale like shapes as shown, and fill with lines.
2. Draw some lines on the petals to create depth.

DONE!

DAHLIA

GUIDE

1. Draw four circles as shown.
2. Divide it into 8.

STEP 1.

1. Draw a small circle in the center.
2. Add lines inside so it looks like a peppermint candy.
3. Draw a few tiny petals staying inside the small guide circle.

STEP 2.

1. Draw 8 petals inside the next guide circle, 1 petal on each line.

STEP 3.

1. Draw 8 more petals inbetween the previous 8 petals, stay inside the guide.
2. Repeat the process with 8 more bigger petals as shown.

STEP 4.

1. Draw slightly wider petals inbetween the previous 8, staying inside the guide.
2. Add little petals in any empty spaces.

STEP 5.

1. Add details petal by petal, concentrate the lines in the center of each petal.

DONE!

DAISIES

GUIDE

1. Draw the outer circle.
2. Mark the center and divide it into 8.
3. Draw another circle in the center about the 1/3 of the diameter.

STEP 1.

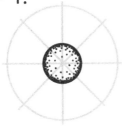

1. Draw a circle around the center guide, and add lots of dots as shown. Make sure to keep center empty.

STEP 2.

1. Draw rounded petals on the diagonal guidelines.

STEP 3.

1. Draw 8 extra petals inbetween the first 8.
2. Add lines on each petal, coming from the center of the flower.

DONE!

GUIDE

1. Draw the outer circle.
2. Mark the center and divide it into 8.
3. Add a small circle in the center.

STEP 1.

1. Draw a bumpy circle in the center as shown.
2. Add some dots inside.

STEP 2.

1. Draw slim pointy petal shapes on the diagonal guidelines.

STEP 3.

1. Add details petal by petal, by drawing lines in the center of each petal coming from the base.
2. Add a few lines at the end of the petals too.

DONE!

21

FORGET ME NOT

GUIDE

1. Draw the outer circle.
2. Add a small circle in the center.
3. Fit 5 more circles inside.
4. Draw 5 diagonal lines as shown.

STEP 1.

1. Draw a tiny circle in the center and surround it with dots.
2. Draw a small 5 petaled flower shape in the center.
3. Add small leaf shapes in the empty spaces as shown.

STEP 2.

1. Draw 5 petal shapes using the guide, giving 2 petals a pointy end and the rest an indented end as shown.

STEP 3.

1. Add details petal by petal, starting with a line in the center of the petal, then add shorter lines around as shown.
2. Repeat for the rest.

DONE!

Put a few flowers together to create a bunch..

GUIDE

1. Draw a curved line as the stem.
2. Add 3 circles overlapping a little.
3. Add some short lines as shown.

STEP 1.

1. Draw a flower inside the circle.
2. Draw circles at the top of the stem, make sure the circles get smaller towards the top.

STEP 2.

1. Draw 2 more flowers in the guide.
2. Fill in the small circles with short lines as shown.
3. Add a leaf at the base.

DONE!

FREESIAS

GUIDE

1. Draw a circle.
2. Mark the center, and divide it into 6 sections.

STEP 1.

Draw 2 rounded petals as shown.

STEP 2.

Add a small curved line in the the center and draw 1 more petal.

STEP 3.

1. Add 3 more petals using the guide.
2. Draw 4 lines coming out of the center, and add a dot to each end.
3. Give it some little details as shown.

DONE!

GUIDE

1. Draw 2 lines on an angle, connected at the base like a long V.
2. Add 2 more diagonal lines on both sides as shown.
3. Connect all 4 lines with a curved line along the top.

STEP 1.

1. Draw a V shape at the base of the guide.
2. Add a little stem shape as shown.
3. Draw 2 petals on both sides using the guide.

STEP 2.

1. Draw a petal in the center, connecting to the previous 2 petals.
2. Add 2 extra petals inbetween the main 3.
3. Add some little details as shown.

DONE!

GUIDE

Follow this guide to put the flowers together.

Make the buds get smaller towards the top.
DONE!

25

GARDENIA

GUIDE

1. Draw the outer circle.
2. Mark the center and divide it into 6.
3. Draw 2 more circles inside as shown.

STEP 1.

1. Draw a line like the top of a question mark.
2. Add a curved line on the left, then add 2 more lines as shown.
3. Draw curved lines inside, following the order shown.
4. Draw a petal with a "fold" on the top.

STEP 2.

1. Draw these bent lines around the center of the flower starting from the top going clockwise.
TIP: Stay close to the middle guide circle as shown.

STEP 3.

1. Turn the lines from STEP 2 into petals. Follow from ①-⑥ to get a nice balance.
2. Add an extra line to some of them to create the folded look.

STEP 4.

1. Add 6 petals on the diagonal guidelines, following the ①-⑥ shown here. Vary the shapes slightly, but stay inside the circle.
2. Add the folded look on some of them.

STEP 5.

1. Add details petal by petal, draw lines at the base of each petal and add some short lines from the edge as shown.

DONE!

GERBERA

GUIDE

1. Draw the outer circle.
2. Mark the center, and draw another circle 1/3 the diameter.
3. Divide the whole thing into 8.
4. Add one more circle in the center.

STEP 1.

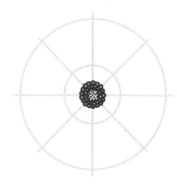

1. Draw 2 layers of tiny circles along the guideline.
2. Fill in the center with dots.

STEP 2.

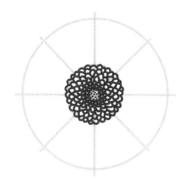

1. Fill in the meddium guide circle with bump like shapes as shown.

STEP 3.

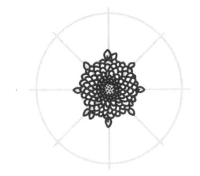

1. Draw small petals on the 8 diagonal guidelines.

STEP 4.

1. Draw rounded petal shapes, starting with 8 on the diagonal guidelines.
2. Fill in any blank spaces with petals.
TIP: Keep the amount of petals and position random for an organic look.

STEP 5.

1. Add details petal by petal, by drawing lines in the center of each petal coming from the base. Leave negative space at the edges of each petal.

DONE!

HIBISCUS

GUIDE

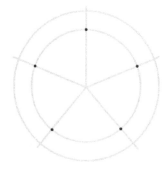

1. Draw the outer circle.
2. Mark the center, and divide it into 5.
TIP: Thinking of a star ★ or a starfish might help to get the right balance.
3. Draw a slightly smaller circle inside and mark where the diagonal lines cross the circle.

STEP 1.

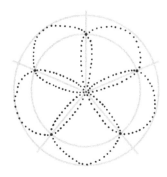

1. Sketch out petal shapes using the guideline as shown.
Make sure the petals cross over at the marked points.

STEP 2.

1. Draw a pistil coming out of the center of the guide.
2. Add 5 tiny circles at the top, then connect them to the pistil with short lines as shown.

STEP 3.

1. Draw short lines underneath the top of the pistil.
2. Add a dot to each end.

STEP 4.

1. Draw these overlapping petal shapes using the sketch from step 1. Make the edges are ruffled as shown.
TIP: Stay inside the circle.

STEP 5.

1. Add details, starting with lines coming out of the center of the flower.
2. Add short lines at the edge, coming from the "ruffles" as shown.

DONE!

IRIS

GUIDE

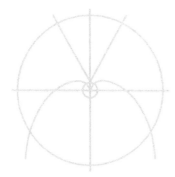

1. Draw a circle and add a line straight through the middle.
2. Mark the center and draw a horizontal line, then add a small circle in the center.
3. Draw 2 diagonal lines on top of the small circle.
4. Add 2 curved lines as shown.

STEP 1.

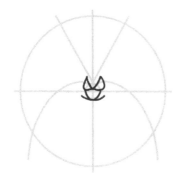

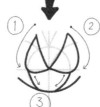

1. Draw a "V" in the center and add a curved line on the guide circle.

2. Add 2 curved lines on the "V", then 2 more lines below as shown.

STEP 2.

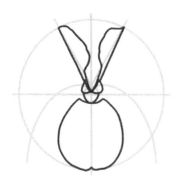

1. Draw these 2 petal shapes along the diagonal guidelines.
2. Add a round petal at the base, the petal is connected to the bottom of STEP 1. Give the petal a little indent at the tip.

STEP 3.

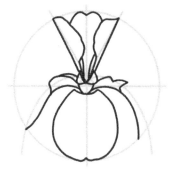

1. Draw a petal shape inbetween the top 2 petals.
2. Add 2 curved lines coming from center of the flower, close to the guide, then add the shapes you see coming from the center, these are the folds of the next petals.

STEP 4.

1. Turn the curved lines from STEP 3 into petals as shown.
TIP: Make the petals look different.

STEP 5.

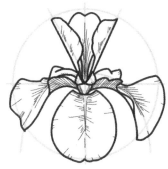

1. Add details petal by petal, starting with the top 3.
2. Draw in the details of the botom petal, use horizontal and vertical lines.
3. Add the details to the side petals as shown.

DONE!

LILY

GUIDE

1. Draw the outer circle.
2. Divide it into 6.

STEP 1.

1. Draw 3 petals using the guideline as shown.

STEP 2.

1. Add 2 more petals at the bottom of the lilly making sure the tip of the petal is facing down.
2, Draw a patel at the top, with a flat end as shown.

STEP 3.

1. Draw 4 lines coming out of the center of the flower.
2. Add small ovals on each end.

STEP 4.

1. Add details petal by petal, by using simple lines as shown.
2. Draw a short line near the top of each petal.

STEP 5.

1. Add some dots around the center of the lily. Vary the size for an organic look.

DONE!

LOTUS

GUIDE

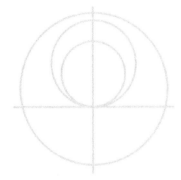

1. Draw the outer circle.
2. Add a vertical line straight through the middle.
3. Draw a horizontal line just below the center.
4. Add 2 more circles as shown.

STEP 1.

1. Draw a rounded petal shape inside the smallest guide circle.
2. Draw two more petals on each side, staying in the guide.
TIP: Make them asymmetrical for an organic look!

STEP 2.

1. Draw a petal inbetween the previous step, then add 2 more petals on each side as shown.
2. Add 2 bigger petals on the left and right, making sure the left petal is bigger.

STEP 3.

1. Add 2 more petals below what you've drawn so far, give the left petal a folded look as shown. Remember to stay inside the guide.

STEP 4.

1. Add 3 more petals at the base, starting with the right hand side.
2. Draw an extra line on the left petal to create the folded look.
3. Add a simple stem.

STEP 5.

1. Add lines at the base of each petal, and also inside the "folds"
2. Add 1 or 2 short lines at the top of each petal.

DONE!

MAGNOLIA

GUIDE

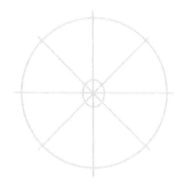

1. Draw the outer circle.
2. Mark the center and divide it into 8.
3. Draw a small oval in the center.

STEP 1.

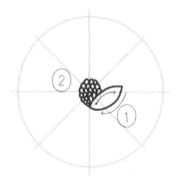

1. Draw a petal at the base of the oval guideline as shown.
2. Fill in the oval guideline with bump shapes.

STEP 2.

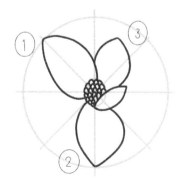

1. Draw a petal using the diagonal guideline on the left.
2. Add another petal on the bottom as shown.
3. Draw 1 more petal but make it smaller this time.

STEP 3.

1. Draw 2 more petals, 1 at the top, and 1 to the right.
2. Add a petal on the left, with an extra line to give it the folded look.

STEP 4.

1. Draw 3 more petals in the empty spaces as shown.
TIP: Stay inside the guide circle.

STEP 5.

1. Add details petal by petal, draw short lines at the base of each petal to create the shadow effect, don't forget to vary the sizes of your lines.

DONE!

ORCHID

GUIDE

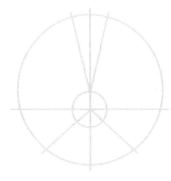

1. Draw the outer circle.
2. Draw a vertical line through the middle.
3. Add a horizontal line in the lower half af the circle.
4. Draw a small circle where the two lines cross.
5. Add 4 diagonal lines as shown.

STEP 1.

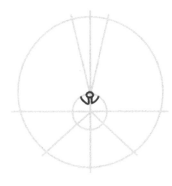

1. Draw a tiny oval on top of the small circle.
2. Add two short lines under the oval.
3. Add 2 curved lines as shown.

STEP 2.

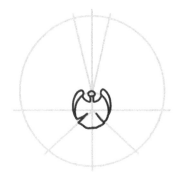

1. Draw wing like shapes along the guideline on the left and right.
2. Add a skirt shape underneath the "wings" staying inside the small circle guide!
3. Add teardrop shapes to the "wings" to create a folded effect.

STEP 3.

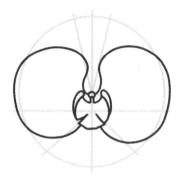

1. Draw 2 big kidney bean shaped petals on both sides, stay close to the outher guide circle.

STEP 4.

1. Draw 3 more petals using the guideline as shown.

STEP 5.

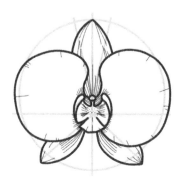

1. Add details petal by petal, start by adding lines and dots to the center.
2. Add small lines at the edge of the big petals as shown.

DONE!

PEONY

GUIDE

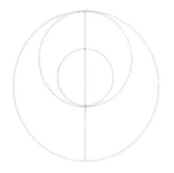

1. Draw a circle and add a line straight through the middle.
2. Draw 2 more circles inside as shown.

STEP 1.

1. Draw 3 petals, starting with the middle one, make sure the petals on the right and left stay inside the guide circle

STEP 2.

1. Add 3 more petals, starting with the left one.
2. Next draw the right one, and finish with the middle petal.
3. The right and left petals need an extra line to create a folded look.

STEP 3.

1. Fill in the center of the flower with more petals as shown.

STEP 4.

1. Draw 5 more petals surrounding the previous steps.
2. Add extra lines to make the petals look folded.

STEP 5.

1. Draw the last 3 petals on the bottom of the peony.
2. Add shading and creases using simple lines to create depth.

DONE!

PLUMERIA

GUIDE

1. Draw a circle.
2. Mark the center and divide it into 5.
TIP: Think of a star ★ or a starfish to help you get the right balance.

STEP 1.

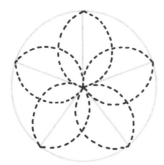

Sketch out these pointed petal shapes very lightly to help with the balance of the petals.

STEP 2.

Draw a curved line on the same side of every petal as shown.

STEP 3.

Connect the top of each curved line to the next, turning them into petals.

STEP 4.

Draw a curved line in each petal from the center, stopping before the end of the petal.

STEP 5.

Add details petal by petal, drawing lines from the center as shown.

DONE!

POPPY

GUIDE

1. Draw the outer circle.
2. Mark the center and divide it into 6.
3. Draw 2 more circles in the center as shown.

STEP 1.

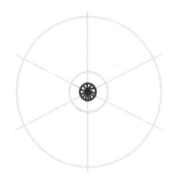

1. Draw a circle in the center using the guide.
2. Add short lines inside it as shown.

STEP 2.

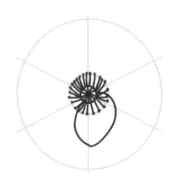

1. Draw lines around STEP 1, staying inside the guide circle.
2. Add dots on the tip of each line.
3. Draw a petal as shown.

STEP 3.

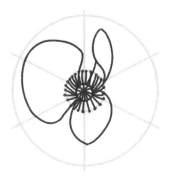

1. Draw a big petal on the left.
2. Combine 3 curved lines to create a folded petal as shown. Make sure these 2 petals don't touch the edge of the guide circle.

STEP 4.

1. Draw a large petal with a ruffled edge on the top, almost taking up half of the guide circle.
2. Add another petal on the bottom right, using the guide to get a nice shape.
3. Draw another large petal on the left and add a small one in the empty space as shown.

STEP 5.

1. Add details petal by petal.
2. Concentrate more lines in the center and vary the line lengths.

DONE!

RED CAMELLIA
(CAMELLIA JAPONICA)

GUIDE

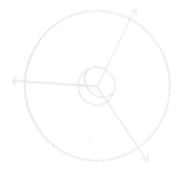

1. Draw the outer circle.
2. Mark the center, and draw 3 lines as shown.
3. Add a circle in the center and a curved line inside, creating a "crescent" shape.

STEP 1.

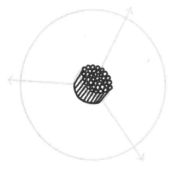

1. Draw little circles in the top half of the guide circle,
Leave the "crescent" section blank.
2. Add lines in the "crescent" section as shown.

STEP 2.

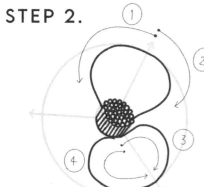

Draw 2 petals on the diagonal guidelines, starting with the big one at the top. Use the guidelines to find center point of each petal.
TIP: Following the ①-④ shown will help you get the nice balance.

STEP 3.

Draw another petal on the left side.

STEP 4.

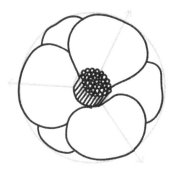

Add 3 petals in the blank space giving them wavy edges as shown. TIP: Stay inside the circle!

STEP 5.

Add details petal by petal, starting with the front 3. use more lines close to the center to create depth.

DONE!

HOW TO DRAW A

ROSE

GUIDE

1. Draw a circle.
2. Add a swirl inside,
slightly off center as shown.

STEP 1.

1. Draw a "Y" in the center.

STEP 2.

1. Fill in the top of the "Y" shape
with little petals as shown.
2. Add one more petal wrapping
around the left of the "Y" shape.

STEP 3.

1. Draw more petal shapes using the swirl as your guide.

STEP 4.

1. Draw a big petal surrounding the center "Y" of the rose.
2. Add one more on top.

STEP 5.

top

bottom

1. Draw 5 outer petals starting with the top and bottom.
2. Add shading and creases with simple lines as shown.

DONE!

SNOWDROP

GUIDE

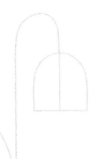

1. Draw a straight line curved at the top and add a bell shape at the end of the line as shown.
2. Add another line at the base, this is going to be a leaf.

STEP 1.

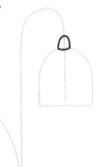

Draw small bell shape at the top of the flower guide.

STEP 2.

Draw these 2 petal shapes inside the flower guide as shown.

STEP 3.

1. Draw a petal inbetween STEP 2, and add 2 lines in the center to create pistils.
2. Draw 2 lines along the stem guide.

STEP 4.

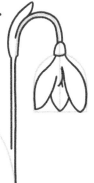

Add a small leaf shape at the top of the stem as shown, then carry on drawing the stem stopping at the bottom leaf guide.

STEP 5.

1. Draw a leaf at the bottom.
2. Add details as shown.

DONE!

HOW TO DRAW A
SUNFLOWER

GUIDE

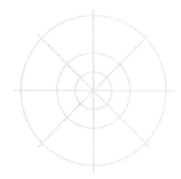

1. Draw the outer circle.
2. Mark the center, and divide it into 8.
3. Add 2 more circles as shown.

STEP 1.

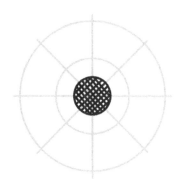

1. Fill the center with cross hatch lines.

STEP 2.

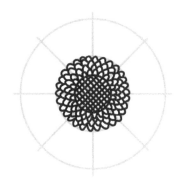

1. Fill in the next guide circle with bump like shapes as shown.

STEP 3.

1. Draw pointy petals on the 8 diagonal guidelines.

STEP 4.

1. Fill in the spaces inbetween the first 8 petals with more petals.
TIP: Keep the shape of the petals consistent and overlap them randomly.

STEP 5.

1. Add details petal by petal, by drawing lines in the center of each petal coming from the base.
2. Add a few lines at the end of petal.

DONE!

CONGRATULATIONS ON MAKING
IT THROUGH ALL 25 GUIDES.

NOW IT'S TIME TO
PRACTICE DRAWING!

USE THE STEP BY STEP GUIDES
AS A REFERENCE IF NEEDED.
JUST HAVE FUN WITH IT :)

PRACTICE
PAGES

NOTES

ANEMONE

STEP BY STEP ON PAGE 6

NOTES

ANTHURIUM

PRACTICE

STEP BY STEP ON PAGE 8

NOTES

BIRD OF PARADISE

PRACTICE

STEP BY STEP ON PAGE 10

CAMELLIA

STEP BY STEP ON PAGE 12

NOTES

CLEMATIS

PRACTICE

 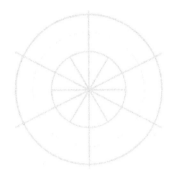

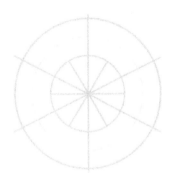 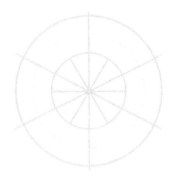

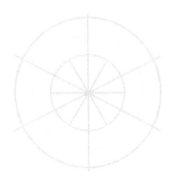 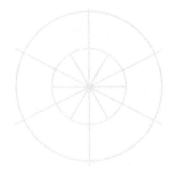

STEP BY STEP ON PAGE 14

NOTES

CORNFLOWER

 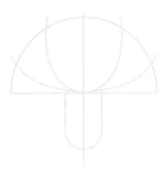

STEP BY STEP ON PAGE 16

NOTES

DAHLIA

PRACTICE

STEP BY STEP ON PAGE 18

NOTES

DAISIES

PRACTICE

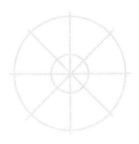

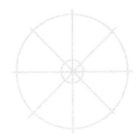

STEP BY STEP ON PAGE 20

NOTES

FORGET ME NOT

STEP BY STEP ON PAGE 22

NOTES

FREESIAS

PRACTICE

STEP BY STEP ON PAGE 24

NOTES

GARDENIA

PRACTICE

STEP BY STEP ON PAGE 26

NOTES

GERBERA

PRACTICE

STEP BY STEP ON PAGE 28

NOTES

HIBISCUS

PRACTICE

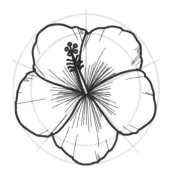
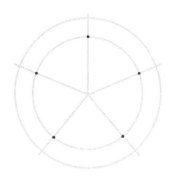

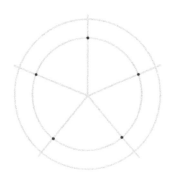
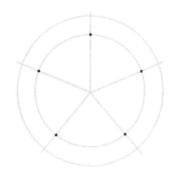

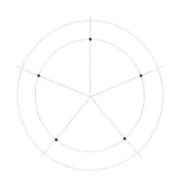

STEP BY STEP ON PAGE 30

NOTES

IRIS

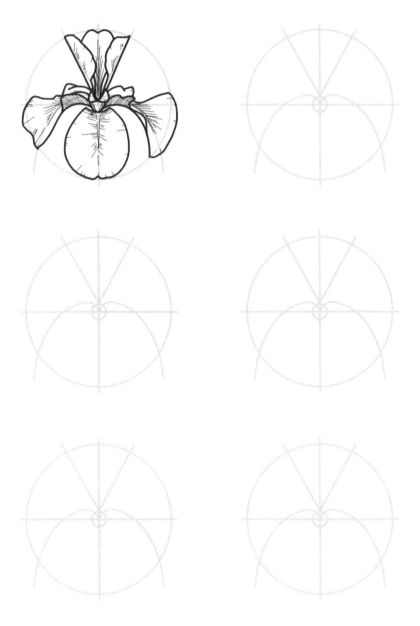

STEP BY STEP ON PAGE 32

NOTES

LILY

PRACTICE

STEP BY STEP ON PAGE 34

NOTES

LOTUS

PRACTICE

STEP BY STEP ON PAGE 36

NOTES

MAGNOLIA

PRACTICE

STEP BY STEP ON PAGE 38

NOTES

ORCHID

PRACTICE

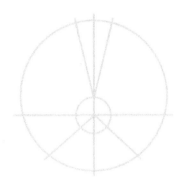
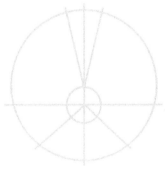
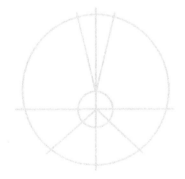
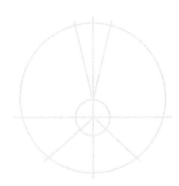
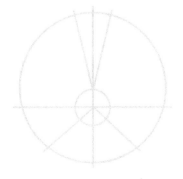

STEP BY STEP ON PAGE 40

NOTES

PEONY

PRACTICE

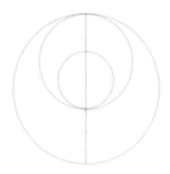

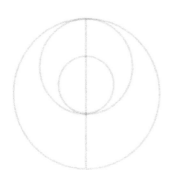
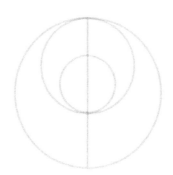

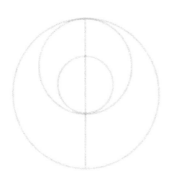
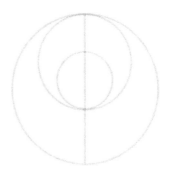

STEP BY STEP ON PAGE 42

NOTES

PLUMERIA

PRACTICE

STEP BY STEP ON PAGE 44

NOTES

POPPY

PRACTICE

STEP BY STEP ON PAGE 46

NOTES

RED CAMELLIA

(CAMELLIA JAPONICA)

P R A C T I C E

 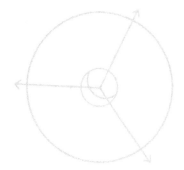

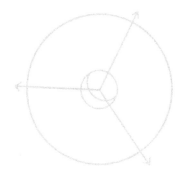 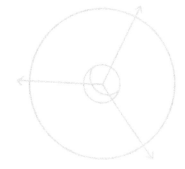

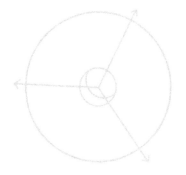 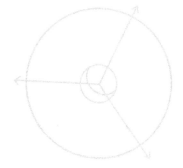

STEP BY STEP ON PAGE 48

NOTES

ROSE

PRACTICE

STEP BY STEP ON PAGE 50

NOTES

SNOWDROP

PRACTICE

STEP BY STEP ON PAGE 52

NOTES

SUNFLOWER

STEP BY STEP ON PAGE 54

Made in the USA
Las Vegas, NV
27 November 2024

12830216R00059